A New True Book

HALLEY'S COMET

By Dennis B. Fradin

DIXON PUBLIC LIBRARY
DIXON, ILLINOIS

CHILDRENS PRESS ®

CHICAGO

Simple telescope used in 1647.

PHOTO CREDITS
Ann Ronan Picture Library—2, 10, 12, 14
National Optical Astronomy Observatories—5, 19, 21, 25 (2 photos), 40
The Bettmann Archive—6, 9
NASA—17, 28, 35, 44
California Institute of Technology—23
Holiday Film Corporation—26 (top), 31, 42
Tony Freeman—26 (bottom)
Candee Productions—32
Fotokhronika TASS—37
ESA European Space Agency—Cover, 38 (top), 39
National Space Development Agency of Japan (NASDA)—38 (bottom)
Nawrocki Stock Photo:
© Robert M. Lightfoot—45

Cover: ESA printing of *Giotto's* encounter with Halley's Comet

For Charlene Roth

Library of Congress Cataloging in Publication Data

Fradin, Dennis B.
  Halley's comet.

  (A New true book)
  Includes index.
  Summary: Describes the general characteristics of comets and gives a brief history of Halley's comet discussing its expected reappearance in late 1985-early 1986.
  1. Halley's comet—Juvenile literature.
[1. Halley's comet. 2. Comets] I. Title.
QB723.H2F7 1985   523.6'4   85-17067
ISBN 0-516-01275-4   AACR2

Copyright ©1985 by Regensteiner Publishing Enterprises, Inc.
All rights reserved. Published simultaneously in Canada.
Printed in the United States of America.
    3 4 5 6 7 8 9 10 R 94 93 92 91 90 89 88 87 86

J
523.6
F841

TABLE OF CONTENTS

Ingraham — 6/88 — 8.8.98(4.00)

141461

HALLEY'S COMET IS COMING!

Once every seventy-six years or so, a lovely comet appears in the night sky. It isn't the brightest comet, nor the largest. But it is the most famous comet. Its name is Halley's Comet.

The chance to see Halley's Comet comes just once in a lifetime for most people. Astronomers study it closely. Even people with

At the Kitt Peak National Observatory a computer was used to add color to this black and white image of Halley's Comet, photographed in 1910 at Lowell Observatory.

no interest in astronomy try to see it. Halley's Comet has been beautiful on past visits, and it probably will be again when it appears in 1985-1986!

5

Galileo demonstrates to the senate of Venice the refracting telescope he built. Galileo was the first scientist to use a telescope to study the skies. In 1610 he discovered that the moon shines with reflected light and that its surface is mountainous, that countless stars make up the Milky Way, that Jupiter has four large satellites, and that sunspots move across the face of the sun.

COMETS IN OLDEN TIMES

People of past centuries feared comets because they didn't know anything about them. Most thought that comets were evil stars or monsters in the sky. When a comet appeared, they thought it meant that some disaster was about to occur.

Any disaster that happened while a comet was in sight was blamed on the "evil star." Nearly four thousand years ago Arabs blamed a comet for a famine. The English thought a comet caused their defeat by William the Conqueror in the year 1066. Even the word *disaster,* meaning "evil star," came from people's fear of certain heavenly bodies, including comets.

THE BEGINNINGS
OF COMET SCIENCE

Ancient people thought
that comets traveled just a
few miles above the earth.
The Danish astronomer
Tycho Brahe (1546-1601)

Tycho
Brahe

Drawing showing the instruments Tycho Brahe used to study the skies.

proved this idea false. While studying a bright comet in 1577, Brahe decided that comets are millions of miles from earth when they appear.

Most astronomers in the late 1500s and early 1600s thought that a comet came once and was never seen again. They thought a comet approached the sun in a straight line, spun around the sun, and then disappeared into space in another straight line.

The great English scientist Isaac Newton (1642-1727) discovered that comets don't move in straight lines. He found

Isaac
Newton

that most move in elliptical (egg-shaped) orbits around the sun. He also found that comets are members of the solar system, like the planets, and that a comet can return again and again.

EDMOND HALLEY'S COMET

The English astronomer Edmond Halley (1656-1742) agreed with his friend Isaac Newton that a comet could return. Halley read about famous comets in history. He studied reports written long before to find comets that came back again and again.

Halley found that one bright comet had appeared in 1531 and another in

Edmond Halley predicted that the comet that he had seen in 1682 would return in 1758. He was right.

1607. In 1682 he himself viewed a bright comet. Halley decided that these weren't three separate comets. Instead, they were one comet that returned about every seventy-six years.

Edmond Halley knew that he wouldn't live to see the comet of 1682 return seventy-six years later. But he wrote: "I would venture confidently to predict its return in the year 1758."

On Christmas night, 1758, on a farm in Germany, Johann Georg Palitzsch spotted a fuzzy patch of light through his homemade telescope. As days passed, the fuzzy patch brightened. It was

the comet Edmond Halley
had said would return in
1758! Because of his
prediction, the comet was
named Halley's Comet.

Astronomers then turned
to historical records. The
oldest definite mention
they found of Halley's
Comet was made by the
Chinese in 240 B.C. The
comet the English blamed
for their defeat in the year
1066 also was found to be
Halley's Comet.

Spacecraft are now used to photograph our solar system. In the picture grouping above you can see Earth as it rises over the moon's surface. The planet Venus is above the moon's surface. From left to right above Venus and Earth are the planets Jupiter, Mercury, Mars, and Saturn.

WHAT IS A COMET?

The sun and all the objects that orbit it are called the solar system. The sun is by far the largest object in the solar system. The planets, moons, meteoroids, and asteroids all belong to the solar system. Comets belong to the solar system, too.

Astronomers call comets "dirty snowballs." That is because they believe a comet's head—its main part—is a ball of ice with dust, gases, metal, and rock frozen inside.

As a comet approaches the sun, the heat melts some of its ice. Dust and

Photograph of the Comet IRAS-Araki-Alcock as it appeared on the night of May 8, 1983. The head of the comet is at the lower left and its tail stretches out behind.

gases fly off the head and fan out. They become the comet's tail. Comets' tails are millions of miles long and always point away from the sun.

Comets have no light of their own. Only when comets are near the sun and are lighted by it can they be seen without a telescope.

A comet's period is the time it takes to orbit the sun. The farther a comet goes from the sun, the longer its period. Most comets have periods of hundreds or even thousands of years.

The Comet IRAS-Araki-Alcock passed within 2.8 million miles of the earth. This was a minor comet, perhaps only one-thousandth the size of Halley's Comet.

A comet's period may vary from one orbit to another. For example, Halley's Comet can take anywhere from seventy-five to seventy-nine years to appear again. This change in travel time occurs because as a comet passes planets their gravity slows the comet down. Other times the pull of their gravity speeds it up. It all depends on a planet's position when the comet passes.

HALLEY'S COMET RETURNS: 1985-1986

Several years before Halley's Comet approached for its 1985-1986 return, astronomers began searching for it. In October 1982 astronomers at California's Palomar

The 200-inch Hale telescope and dome at Palomar Observatory

DIXON PUBLIC LIBRARY
DIXON, ILLINOIS

Observatory found it with
their giant telescope. The
comet was quite dim
because it was still a
billion miles from the sun.

As time passed, Halley's
Comet moved closer to the
sun and became brighter.
In January 1985 it zoomed
past the orbit of the giant
planet Jupiter. The comet
had reached a speed of

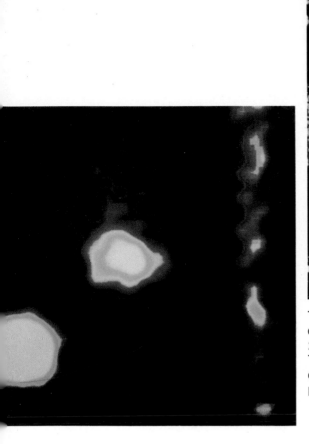

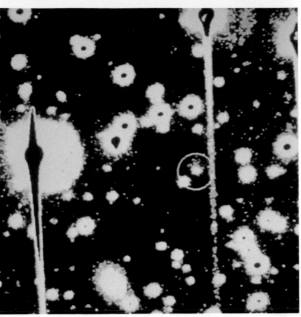

Two computer-enhanced photographs
of Halley's Comet taken September
25, 1984 at Kitt Peak Observatory.
The head of the comet is in the center
of the photograph (left). In the
picture above, Halley's Comet is circled.

3,500 miles per hour and
was still speeding up as it
approached the sun. By
May 1985 the comet was
just 350 million miles from
the sun.

Halley's Comet is due to pass through the star cluster the Pleiades in the constellation Taurus in November 1985. Telescopes (right) are used to study the stars.

Scientists have plotted its orbit so carefully that they know when it should come into view. By mid-November 1985, Halley's Comet should be visible with a small telescope. On the night of November 16-17, 1985, it will be located in the constellation Taurus, just south of the Pleiades star cluster.

The red line shows the path of Halley's Comet. The yellow line shows
the path of the *Venera* spacecraft that will photograph the comet.
The green line shows the orbit of Venus and the blue line shows
the orbit of Earth. Details of *Venera* are shown in corners of the picture.

In early December 1985 someone probably will become the first to spot Halley's Comet without a telescope. It will then be in the constellation Pisces. For about the next five-and-a-half months the comet can be seen with the naked eye. However, it will be visible at different times and in different places.

A good time for people in the Northern Hemisphere to see the comet will be shortly after sunset the week of January 19-25, 1986. It will be located low in the western sky.

Those in the Southern Hemisphere will get the best view of all. In April 1986 the comet will be almost overhead before

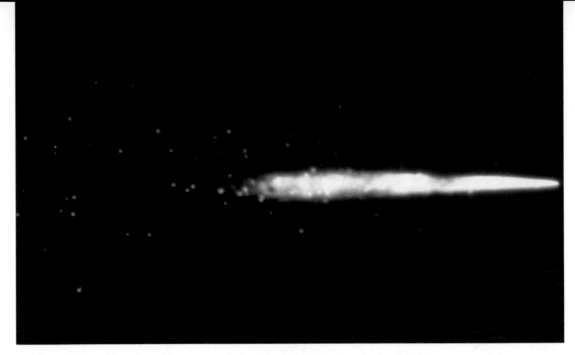

Halley's Comet

dawn for observers in
southern Africa, southern
South America, and
Australia. The comet
should be very bright and
have a long, beautiful tail.

There's a much better
chance to see the comet

The moon is about 238,857 miles away from Earth.

in the country than in the
city. Lights and air
pollution in cities make it
hard to spot objects in the
night sky.

SCIENTIFIC STUDIES OF HALLEY'S COMET

When it appears in 1985-1986, Halley's will be the most thoroughly studied comet of all time. Astronomers will view it from the ground. Halley's will also be the first comet studied up close by spacecraft.

The point where a comet
is nearest the sun is
called its perihelion. At
perihelion a comet is at its
brightest. When Halley's
Comet reaches perihelion
on February 9, 1986, it will
be about fifty-five million
miles from the sun. At that
time the United States will
study it with the *Pioneer
Venus Orbiter,* a
spacecraft now orbiting
Venus.

Drawing of the *Pioneer Venus Orbiter* above the clouds covering Venus

In March 1986 two
Russian spacecraft, *Vega 1*
and *Vega 2,* will fly within
six thousand miles of the
comet. *Giotto,* a spacecraft
built by the European
Space Agency, will make

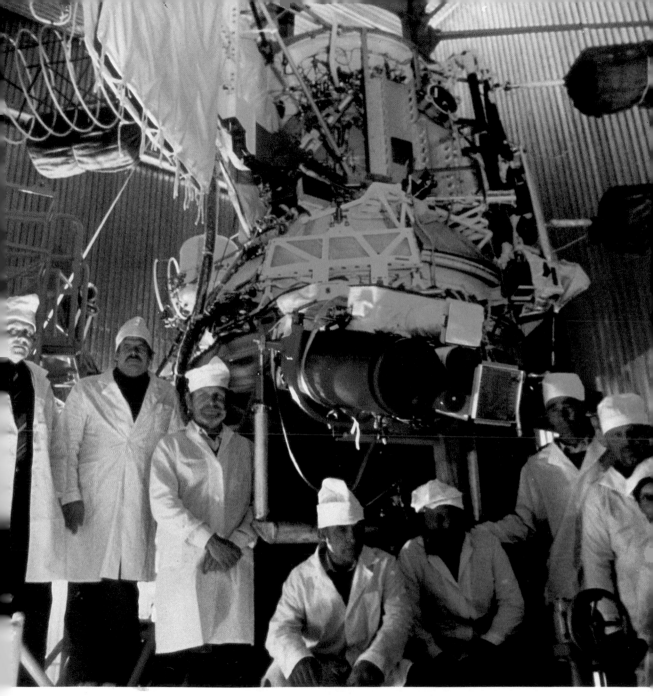

Specialists from the Soviet Union, Bulgaria, Hungary, German Democratic Republic, Poland, Czechoslovakia, Austria, France, and the Federal Republic of Germany developed the *Vega* spacecraft to study Halley's Comet.

Giotto (right) was built by the European Space Agency. Japan's spacecraft (below) is named Planet A.

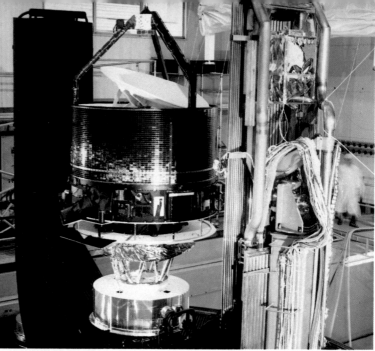

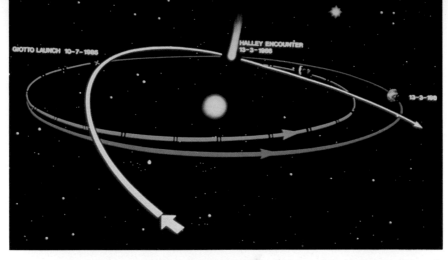

Drawing showing *Giotto's* encounter with Halley's Comet.

the closest approach of all.
In March 1986 *Giotto* will
study Halley's Comet from
less than three hundred
miles away. Japan also is
sending two space
vehicles up to the comet.

These spacecraft will
gather much information
about Halley's Comet.

A color-coded image of Comet West photographed
March 8, 1976. The tail of the comet is driven
away from its head by solar wind.

Scientists then hope to
find out if comets really
are "dirty snowballs." They
also hope to learn how
comets were formed. That
information could help

scientists understand how the entire solar system was formed.

In late spring of 1986, Halley's Comet will fade from view as it heads back out into space. Scientists may not have another chance to study a major comet closely until the year 2061, when Halley's Comet returns.

Comet Ikeya-Seki (opposite page) appeared in 1963.

WILL YOU
DISCOVER A COMET?

Halley's is just one of two thousand known comets. There are probably thousands more undiscovered ones. Comets are named for their discoverers. Comet Ikeya was discovered by nineteen-year-old Kaoru Ikeya of Japan in 1963. In

Comet Kohoutek appeared in 1974.

1968 a sixteen-year-old
Texan named Mark
Whitaker discovered a
comet that was named for
him.

If you buy or make a
small telescope, you might
want to hunt for comets.
Wouldn't it be fun to have
a comet named for you,
just like Edmond Halley?

WORDS YOU SHOULD KNOW

asteroids (AST • er • oydz) — rocky objects located between Mars and Jupiter

astronomers (ast • RON • ih • merz) — persons who study stars, planets, and other heavenly bodies

billion (BILL • yun) — a thousand million (1,000,000,000)

comets (KAH • mets) — objects made of ice, dust, metal, gases, and rock that have long, glowing tails when near the sun

constellation (kahn • stel • AY • shun) — a star group in a certain area of the sky

elliptical (eh • LIP • tih • kil) — egg-shaped

gravity (GRAV • ih • tee) — the force that holds us down to earth and causes one heavenly body to attract another

head (of a comet) (HED) — the part that contains a comet's most solid material

meteoroids (ME • tee • or • oydz) — particles of stone or metal in the solar system

million (MILL • yun) — a thousand thousand (1,000,000)

moons (MOONZ) — natural objects that orbit the planets

Northern Hemisphere (NOR • thirn HEM • iss • feer) — the northern half of the world

orbit (OR • bit) — the path an object takes when it moves around another object

perihelion (pare • ih • HEEL • ee • on) — the closest approach to the sun by an object in the solar system

period (of a comet) (PEER • ee • ud) — the time a comet takes to complete one orbit around the sun

planet (PLAN • it) — an object that orbits a star

solar system (SO • ler SISS • tim) — the sun and all objects that orbit it

Southern Hemisphere (SUH • thirn HEM • iss • feer) — the southern half of the world

sun (SUHN) — the star closest to the earth

tail (of a comet) (TAYLE) — the trail of dust and gases that fans out from the comet's head

telescopes (TEL • ih • skohpes) — instruments that make distant objects look closer

INDEX

Dennis Fradin would like to hear from you if you get to view Halley's Comet. He would also like to see any drawings you might make of the comet. Write him in care of Childrens Press, 1224 W. Van Buren, Chicago, Illinois 60607

About the Author

Dennis Fradin attended Northwestern University on a partial creative writing scholarship and graduated in 1967. He has published stories and articles in such places as Ingenue, The Saturday Evening Post, Scholastic, Chicago, Oui, *and* National Humane Review. *His previous books include the Young People's Stories of Our States series for Childrens Press, and* Bad Luck Tony *for Prentice-Hall. In the True book series Dennis has written about astronomy, farming, comets, archaeology, movies, Skylab, the space lab, voting and elections, explorers, and pioneers. He is married and the father of three children.*

DIXON PUBLIC LIBRARY

3 1515 00062 6838